10/09

W9-BNX-445

Geography Zone: Landforms™

Exploring
ISLANDS

Melody S. Mis

PowerKiDS
press™

New York

To Mac and Ann Heavener and their family

Published in 2009 by The Rosen Publishing Group, Inc.
29 East 21st Street, New York, NY 10010

First Edition

Editor: Nicole Pristash
Book Design: Julio Gil
Photo Researcher: Jessica Gerweck

Photo Credits: Cover, pp. 5, 19 Shutterstock.com; p. 7 © iStockphoto.com/Klaas Lingbeek- van Kranen; p. 9 (main) Image Courtesy of Earth Sciences and Image Analysis Laboratory, NASA Johnson Space Center; p. 9 (inset) © iStockphoto.com/Peeter Viisimaa; p. 11 © Popperfoto/Getty Images; p. 13 © iStockphoto.com/narvikk; p. 15 © Ira Block/Getty Images; p. 17 © National Geographic/Getty Images; p. 21 © iStockphoto.com/stockcam.

Library of Congress Cataloging-in-Publication Data

Mis, Melody S.
   Exploring islands / Melody S. Mis. — 1st ed.
       p. cm. — (Geography zone. Landforms)
     ISBN 978-1-4358-2712-7 (library binding) — ISBN 978-1-4358-3110-0 (pbk.)
ISBN 978-1-4358-3116-2 (6-pack)
   1. Islands—Juvenile literature. I. Title.
   GB471.M57 2009
   551.42—dc22
                                                            2008024462

Manufactured in the United States of America

Contents

An island is a piece of land that is **surrounded** by water. Islands can be found all over the world. In fact, no one knows how many there are! Some islands are in oceans, and others are in lakes and rivers. Did you know that Manhattan in New York City is an island? The countries of Ireland and Cuba are islands, too.

Islands are some of the world's coolest landforms. Let's learn about the different types of islands and how they are formed. Let's also take a look at some of the most beautiful islands on Earth.

Manhattan is surrounded by the Hudson River, the East River, and the Harlem River. The Williamsburg Bridge, shown here, crosses the East River.

Many people mix continents up with islands. Continents are the seven largest pieces of land on Earth. For example, North America and Africa are continents. Even though they are surrounded by water, as islands are, these places are called continents.

What is the difference between an island and a continent? An island is smaller in size. Greenland is the world's biggest island. Greenland measures around 840,000 square miles (2.2 **million** sq km). Australia is the smallest continent. It measures 2.9 million square miles (7.5 million sq km). Islands come in many shapes and sizes. They are formed in different ways, too.

Part of the coast of Greenland, shown here, is made up of snow-covered mountains and pieces of broken ice called icebergs.

There are chiefly two types of islands. The first is a continental island. A continental island is an island that sits on the same **continental shelf** as a nearby continent. This type of island can be very big. New Guinea, off Australia, and Greenland, off North America, are examples of large continental islands.

Another type of island is an oceanic island. Oceanic islands can be found far away from the mainland or right near a coast. The Hawaiian Islands are examples of oceanic islands. What makes oceanic islands different from continental islands is that oceanic islands are formed by **volcanoes**.

Sable Island is a continental island off the coast of Canada. *Inset:* This is the coast of Sicily, which is one of Italy's continental islands.

Volcanic islands are oceanic islands made from underwater volcanoes. When an underwater volcano **erupts**, **lava** flows out of it. The lava cools, and over time it slowly builds up. This makes the volcano grow bigger. Some volcanoes grow so tall that they rise up above the water. When this happens, they become oceanic islands. In 1963, Surtsey Island, in Iceland, rose up out of the sea and became a new oceanic island.

Sometimes, the volcanoes on volcanic islands remain active. That means they can still erupt. Kilauea volcano on Hawaii's Big Island is the world's most active volcano.

This picture shows the cloud of smoke that rose after the underwater volcanic eruption that formed Surtsey Island in 1963.

A **coral** island is another type of oceanic island. A coral island is made from coral **reefs** that have grown on an underwater volcanic island. Reefs are made from coral polyps. Polyps are tiny animals, and their bones are made of **limestone**. When the polyps die, their bones are left behind. Over time, these bones pile up to form a reef. If the top of the reef grows above the ocean, the reef becomes a coral island.

There are many coral islands in the South Pacific Ocean. Some of them make up the Great Barrier Reef, in Australia.

This is an atoll in the Indian Ocean. An atoll is a coral-reef island that surrounds a small body of water, called a lagoon.

A barrier island is a type of continental island. Barrier islands are long, narrow pieces of land that lie beside a larger piece of land. They are **separated** from the larger land by water. For example, Padre Island, in Texas, is a barrier island.

Barrier islands form when rivers carry sand to the ocean. Ocean waves then carry the sand back near the shore, and the sand piles up to make a mound. When a mound grows and rises above the ocean, it becomes a barrier island. Barrier islands are important because they help keep the coast safe from bad storms.

The Outer Banks, shown here, is a string of barrier islands off the coast of North Carolina that is around 200 miles (322 km) long.

Islands are home to rich animal and plant life. The plants and animals living on continental islands are like those that live on the mainland. Mice, rabbits, snakes, and frogs are common. Crabs, shrimp, and jellyfish are, too.

Animal and plant life on oceanic islands is often very different from life seen on continental islands. Some oceanic islands have plants and animals that are not found anywhere else. Warm oceanic islands have unique, or special, flowers and fruit. Many oceanic islands are known for their birds. The coral islands along the Great Barrier Reef are known for their colorful fish.

These are thick-billed murres. This type of seabird flies to St. George Island, in Alaska, to lay its eggs and have baby birds.

The Hawaiian Islands, in the Pacific Ocean, are full of life and beauty. Colorful flowers, such as hibiscus, jasmine, and orchid, grow there. Umbrella trees and bananas are also plentiful in Hawaii. The islands are also known for having the only **tropical** rain forest in the United States.

The Hawaiian Islands are made up of 8 large islands and more than 100 small islands. Volcanoes formed them millions of years ago. In fact, the Big Island, in Hawaii, is still growing! This is because two volcanoes, Mauna Loa and Kilauea, are still active today.

This is Waikiki Beach, on the island of Oahu, Hawaii. Like many of Hawaii's beaches, Waikiki Beach is a common place for people to visit.

The Galápagos Islands are another group of islands known for their beauty and wildlife. Millions of years ago, volcanoes erupted in the Pacific Ocean near South America. The volcanoes grew and formed the Galápagos Islands. Today, 19 volcanic islands are part of the Galápagos.

The Galápagos are famous for their animals. Some of their animals are not found anyplace else. The islands are named after their giant **tortoises**. *Galápagos* means "giant tortoises" in Spanish. Lizards, penguins, and birds also live there. The most famous Galápagos bird is the blue-footed boobie. It likes to dance on its large blue feet!

The giant tortoise, shown here, can weigh as much as 660 pounds (299 kg)!

People enjoy islands just as animals do. Islands are common places for people to live and to visit. Many islands have warm weather, so people enjoy outdoor activities, such as fishing, swimming, and looking for shells, on them. Many people go diving, too, to see all the colorful things that live in the ocean.

Islands are special landforms. It is fun to learn how they are formed. Maybe you will step foot on an island someday. If you do, think about what made the land you are standing on, and enjoy what the island has to offer!

Glossary

continental shelf (kon-tuh-NEN-tul SHELF) A flat part of the ocean floor near a coastline.

coral (KOR-ul) Hard matter made up of the bones of tiny sea animals.

erupts (ih-RUPTS) Breaks open.

lava (LAH-vuh) Hot, melted rock that comes out of a volcano.

limestone (LYM-stohn) A soft kind of rock.

million (MIL-yun) A thousand thousands.

reefs (REEFS) Strips of coral just under the water.

separated (SEH-puh-rayt-ed) In a different place from something else.

surrounded (suh-ROWND-ed) Having something on all sides.

tortoises (TOR-tus-ez) Turtles that live on land.

tropical (TRAH-puh-kul) Having to do with the warmest parts of Earth.

volcanoes (vol-KAY-nohz) Openings that sometimes shoot up lava.

Index

Web Sites

Due to the changing nature of Internet links, PowerKids Press has developed an online list of Web sites related to the subject of this book. This site is updated regularly. Please use this link to access the list:
www.powerkidslinks.com/gzone/island/